# Embraced *by* God

## Seven Promises for Every Woman

*A Bible Study by*
# BABBIE MASON

## Leader Guide
### Jenny Youngman, Contributor

ABINGDON PRESS
Nashville

EMBRACED BY GOD
Seven Promises for Every Woman Leader Guide

Babbie Mason

*Copyright © 2012 by Abingdon Press*

*This book is printed on acid-free paper.*

ISBN 978-1-4267-5440-1

12 13 14 15 16 17 18 19 20 21 — 10 9 8 7 6 5 4 3 2 1

MANUFACTURED IN THE UNITED STATES OF AMERICA

# CONTENTS

# INTRODUCTION

Embraced by God is an eight-week Bible study designed to help you understand with greater clarity God's deep, sweet love for you and to experience this love as never before. The message is that God not only loves you . . . *you are His favorite!* He loves you as if you were the only one to love.

My eyes were opened to this profoundly new and life-changing understanding of God's love a few years ago when, in a church service I attended, I was invited to say to my neighbor, "I am God's favorite." Now, I was raised in church, a preacher's daughter turned Christian singer, songwriter, and recording artist. I've celebrated my year of jubilee—50 years of being saved and following Jesus. I've always known deep down that God loves me—and that was enough for me. But the idea that I could *ever* be God's favorite seemed to be overstepping a boundary. The thought seemed even a bit presumptuous. This motivated me to seek the truth of His word, and what I discovered is . . . *it's absolutely true!*

Jesus said, "I will be in them and you will be in me so that they will be completely one. Then the world will know that you sent me and that you loved them just *as much as you loved me.*" (John 17:23 NCV, emphasis added). As I've pondered this verse and other passages in John 17, I have come to realize that *God truly loves me as much as He loves Jesus.* And God loves *you* just as much as He loves Jesus!

Through this study you'll lead other women in discovering that they, too, are God's favorite and are loved by God just as much as He loves Jesus. Over the next eight weeks, together you will be embraced by God's love as you explore seven promises He makes to us as His beloved daughters. Each of these promises addresses a specific area in our love relationship with the Lord:

1. You Are Loved Unconditionally by God
2. You Are Beautiful to God
3. You Are Never Alone
4. You Have Everything You Need in God
5. You Have a God-given Purpose
6. You Can Accomplish Great Things in God's Name
7. You Are Equipped With Unique Gifts and Talents

You also will consider how, with the power of Jesus Christ operating within us, we can apply these beautiful aspects of His love in our daily lives. Each week you will study and reflect on one specific promise, with a final week pulling it all together and sending you onward with the challenge to live *loved*.

## About the Participant Book

Prior to your first meeting, you will need to deliver participant books to everyone in your group. They will need to complete the first week of readings *before* your first group session. For each week there are five devotional readings that begin with a Scripture verse and feature the following segments:

| | |
|---|---|
| **Think About His Love** | A devotional reflection that helps you to meditate on the promise and consider how it relates to your life. |
| **Read About His Love** | A guided study of Scripture with space for recording your responses. |
| **Pray About His Love** | Prayer suggestions with a sample prayer to guide you into your own conversation with God. |
| **Be About His Love** | Questions and activities to help you put your love walk into practice. |

Each daily reading can be completed in approximately 20-30 minutes. Completing these readings each week will prepare the women for the discussion and activities of the group session.

## About This Leader Guide

Each week you will gather with the members of your group to watch a video and discuss what you're learning. Sharing how the truths of God's Word are changing your lives will help group members to grow in their ability to receive and share God's love, dramatically impacting every area of their lives. Try to create a warm and welcoming atmosphere in your meeting space, and make sure there is a television and DVD player with working remotes. If you wish, you may choose to provide snacks the first time and invite ladies to rotate bringing refreshments each week.

This leader guide and the DVD will be your primary tools for leading each group session. In this book you will find outlines for eight group sessions, each formatted for a 60-minute session with extended options for a 90-minute gathering (additional time with or without an additional activity). Each session plan follows this format:

**Leader Preparation** (Before the Session)

For your preparation prior to the group session, this section provides a Scripture focus, commentary on the key Bible story, a teaching objective, and a list of materials needed. Read this ahead of time and be prepared to share any of this information as the discussion dictates.

**Warm Up to His Love** (10 minutes; Extended Option 15 minutes)

Each session opens with a welcoming activity, which provides a simple get-to-know-you question intended to help participants engage in the topic and feel comfortable with one another. Extended options are provided for a 90-minnute session.

After this, you will lead the women in reciting John 17:23 together, the memory verse for the study. Hiding this profound truth deep in your hearts will help you to live with the joy of knowing you are loved relentlessly and without exception or condition. The New Century Version of this verse is recommended; however, if your group prefers another translation, you may choose to memorize the verse in that translation. Next you will read aloud an opening prayer. Or, if you prefer, you may choose to pray a prayer of your own or invite different volunteers to pray each week.

Finally, this opening segment concludes with a recap of the week's readings. You may choose to read these aloud to the group, write them on a board or chart, or simply refer to them for your own personal review and preparation for group discussion.

**Bask in His Love** (15-20 minutes)

After you have welcomed the women, recited Scripture, and prayed together, it's time to watch the week's video segment. Be sure to direct participants to the Video Viewer Guide in the participant book, which they may complete as they watch the video.

**Talk About His Love** (20 minutes; Extended Option 30 minutes)

This segment provides discussion points and questions to help you facilitate group discussion. Before the session, choose the discussion points and questions you want to cover, ponder each one, and make some notes in the margins to share in your discussion time. Depending on the number of women in your group and the level of participation, you may not have time to discuss every point or question you have selected; that is OK. Let the Spirit lead and be open to where He takes the conversation. You may read the discussion points aloud or communicate them in your own words; then use the questions that follow to guide your conversation. Those questions that are highlighted in bold may be found in the participant book. For these questions, you may want to invite participants to share the answers they wrote in their books.

**Be About His Love** (5 minutes; Extended Option 10 minutes)

After group discussion, you will invite each woman to turn to a neighbor and discuss a particular challenge from the Be About His Love section of the weekly readings. This will encourage the women to apply what they are discovering to their daily lives and have some accountability.

**Embrace His Love** (5 minutes; Extended Option 10-15 minutes)

To close each session, you will play a selected music video found on the DVD and then lead a time of prayer. Encourage the women to prayerfully meditate on the lyrics or sing along. Extended options for prayer and worship are also provided.

## Before You Begin

Thank you for giving your time, effort, prayers, and dedication to lead others into a deeper love relationship with the Lord. Your leadership is an invaluable investment in their lives and in God's Kingdom work.

God also has something just for *you* on this journey. Allow yourself not only to lead but also to participate fully in the experience. Even as you encourage the women in your group to give God permission to transform their thinking, open yourself to the new understandings and growth God has in store just for *you*.

Be assured that, whatever may be going on in your own life or the world around you, God's loving presence is with you and will empower you to encourage the hearts of the women in your group and guide them into His loving embrace. And as you do, you will come to realize as never before that you are deeply loved, tremendously blessed, and highly favored.

*Babbie*

# Week 1

# YOU ARE LOVED
# UNCONDITIONALLY BY GOD

## Leader Preparation (Before the Session)

**Scripture Focus**

*"I have given these people the glory that you gave me so that they can be one, just as you and I are one. I will be in them and you will be in me so that they will be completely one. Then the world will know that you sent me and that you loved them just as much as you loved me."*

John 17:22-23 NCV

**Key Bible Story**

If we want to begin our discovery of God's great and deep love for His children, we need look no further than Jesus' prayer right before His arrest. Jesus had just washed the feet of His disciples. He had shared a Passover meal with them and taught them the final things He wanted them to know before His death. After He taught them, He went to pray.

In John 17, we see Jesus praying for His disciples—for you and for me. The amazing thing about this prayer was that it was a family prayer. Jesus intercedes for His brothers and His sisters and in doing so, shows us that believers are part of the family. He prays that those who believe in and follow after Him would know the reality and the presence of God's love as He does. In fact, Jesus prays that God would confirm in the hearts of believers that we would know God loves us as much as He loved Jesus. Meditate for a moment on this truth: *God loves us just as much as He loves Jesus.*

Today, in your session you will focus on God's unconditional love for us. This truth is often hard to take in, but right here in John 17 we see that God loves us as much as He loves His own Son.

**Objective**

Today you'll help your group to discover the amazing, unconditional love of God as they consider that God loves them as much as He loves Jesus.

**What You Will Need**
- *Embraced by God* DVD and DVD player
- Bookmark-size strips of colored cardstock paper and fine-tip markers (for Be About His Love Extended Option)

# Notes

## Warm Up to His Love (10 minutes; Extended Option 15 minutes)

### Welcome Activity

For your first session, you will want to make sure that your group has a chance to get to know one another. Go around the room and have everyone briefly introduce herself and share one area in which she hopes to grow or discover something new through your time together in the coming weeks.

### *Extended Option*

Ask participants to think of a sweet love story they have experienced in their lives. Perhaps it was when they were in elementary school and received a playground marriage proposal, or maybe someone is living out a current day love story. Invite volunteers to share their stories.

### Recite the Memory Verse

Share with the group that throughout the study you will work to memorize John 17:23 so that you can hide this encouraging truth deep in your hearts and live with the joy of knowing you are loved unconditionally by God. For ease in reciting, make sure you are memorizing the same translation. The New Century Version is printed here and in the participant book. If your group prefers another translation, you may choose to memorize the passage in that translation of the Bible.

For the first week, read the verse aloud together. You may want to write it on a marker board or flip chart.

*"I will be in them and you will be in me so that they will be completely one. Then the world will know that you sent me and that you loved them just as much as you loved me."*

John 17:23 NCV

### Opening Prayer

Pray this prayer or one of your own to begin your study today:

*Dear heavenly Father,*

*Thank You for Your unconditional love. We confess that we have a hard time understanding unconditional love, and we sure have a hard time giving it away sometimes. So, Lord, today we thank You for illuminating Your word. We are humbled that we can know the love You have for us is the same love You have for Your Son, Jesus. We are forever changed and eternally grateful. We pray in His precious name. Amen.*

### Weekly Reading Recap

- You are God's favorite. The Bible is like a love letter from God to you, telling you all about God's great, unconditional, and unstoppable love for you.
- No matter how far away from God we think we are or how far we think we have fallen, we can always start again. God will always, always wipe the slate clean when we turn to Him for a new beginning.

# Notes

- In order to grow in our love relationship with God, we have to tend our hearts like soil in a garden. We also have to guard our hearts from the snares of the enemy.
- Whatever we may have heard about our worth, we matter to God. We are significant to God. God knit us together and formed us with great care.
- When you feel overlooked, ignored, or invisible, remember that God knows your name. He even knows the sound of your voice.

## Bask in His Love (15-20 minutes)

Play the Week 1 video segment on the DVD. Invite participants to complete the Video Viewer Guide for Week 1 in the participant book as they watch.

## Talk About His Love (20 minutes; Extended Option 30 minutes)

**Discussion Points**
1. Human love is temperamental, temporary, and tentative. God's love is perfect, unconditional, sacrificial, invincible, and never-ending.
   - What are some examples of ways that we are temperamental, temporary, and tentative with our love?
   - What are some examples of the way God's love is perfect, unconditional, sacrificial, invincible, and never-ending?

2. God not only has the ability to love; He is Love personified. Ask a volunteer to read aloud 1 John 4:7-8.
   - What does John say about God in this passage?
   - What does the passage say about the very nature and character of God?
   - What does the passage teach us about how to live as God's beloved?

3. Ask who in the group can recite John 3:16 from memory. Say the verse aloud together. Talk together about how old you were when you learned this verse. Point out that sometimes we gloss over enormous truths such as the fact that God loves us. We hear it; we read it; we think we know it. But when we really ponder that truth, most of us struggle to fully believe it.
   - What did it feel like to write your name into the verse this week? Were you moved? Awed? Did it feel awkward or too good to be true?
   - How does reading the Bible like a love letter from God help us come to know God's love more deeply?
   - **How is your life changed because of God's love for you?** (See Day 1.)

4. It doesn't matter who you are or what your story may be. You can start again. Jesus will forgive every mistake, and He can satisfy every longing you have, if you ask Him. Everybody can use a do-over every now and then—another opportunity to get things right with the Lord.

# Notes

- When have you needed a do-over?
- How have you experienced God's grace to start again after a time of trial, temptation, or rebellion—or even just after a really bad day?
- **What fresh start do you need to make today?** (See Day 2.)

5. A farmer knows what it's like each year to begin again. Jesus uses the art of comparison as He tells the story of the sower in Matthew 13. Invite a volunteer to read aloud Matthew 13:1-9, 18-23.
   - **What happened to the seeds on the path?** What does Jesus say about the person who hears God's Word but doesn't understand it?
   - **What happened to the seeds in the rocks?** What does Jesus say about the person who hears the Word but has a stony heart?
   - **What happened to the seeds in the thorns?** What does Jesus say about the one who hears the Word, but whose heart is filled with compromise?
   - **What happened to the seeds on the good soil?** What happens to the one who hears God's Word, understands it, and does what it says?
   - **Would you say your heart is more like the path, the rocks, the thorns, or the good soil today?** In other words, are you lacking understanding, do you have a stony heart, are you filled with compromise, or are you thriving and flourishing with Jesus?
   - **How can you till the soil of your heart so that God's work can sink in deep and grow roots that produce an abundant harvest of love, faith, joy, and life?** (See Day 3.)

6. You matter to God. God created you because He loves you, and He wants to express His great love for the world through you. Try to wrap your mind around that truth for a moment. The God of the universe created you intentionally, with a purpose and destiny in mind, so that He could love you, be loved by you, and express His love through you.
   - When you imagine God loving the world through you, what comes to mind?
   - When have you felt God working in you to express His love through you?
   - How does the knowledge that God created you for a purpose inspire you to live with intention and boldness?

7. Do not confuse what others have said about you with what God says about you. And do not confuse how they feel about you with how God sees you: You are loved. You are treasured. You are accepted. You are redeemed. You are gifted. You are unequalled. You are preferred. You are blessed. You are favored.
   - How can negative messages from others—or even from our own self-talk—tear us down and make us question our worth?
   - Why do we often believe the lies that the enemy tries to make us believe?
   - What can we do to refuse those negative messages and claim the promise that we matter to God—that God formed us and favors us?

# Notes

8. Take some time to read God's promises of love and care for His children. Assign the following passages to volunteers: 2 Corinthians 5:17, Matthew 11:28-30, Ephesians 3:20, James 1:4, Proverbs 4:23, Galatians 6:9, Jeremiah 1:5a, Psalm 139:15-16, Ephesians 1:4-5. Discuss what each verse teaches us about God's unconditional love.
   - When we feel unnoticed, overlooked, and ignored, how can these promises keep us from feeling worthless or insignificant?
   - You are loved unconditionally by God. Name some words that come to mind when you consider God's unconditional love for you.
   - Invite each participant to complete the following statement: **"I matter to God because…"** (See Day 4.) Tell them that they will have the opportunity to talk more about this with a partner in a few minutes.

9. Living to please God is the primary reason you were born. You were created to bring God glory with your life.
   - Read aloud John 6:1-13. What was the miracle? What is your immediate reaction to the fact that the boy didn't receive recognition?
   - **What is in your "basket" that God can use?** (See Day 5.)

## Be About His Love (5 minutes; Extended Option 10 minutes)

Ask everyone to turn to a neighbor to talk about a particular challenge from the Be About His Love section of the weekly readings. Say something like this: *On Day 4 you discovered that you matter to God. As you ended your daily reading, you were invited to write "I matter" statements. Talk with your partner about how easy or difficult it was to consider why you matter to God, and how that experience helped you understand more fully God's love for you and challenged you to live with purpose.*

### Extended Option
Hand out bookmark-size strips of colored cardstock paper and fine-tip markers to participants. Invite them to create a bookmark that will remind them of God's promise to love them unconditionally. They may want to write their "I Matter" statements on the bookmark or list the promises from the Scriptures you discussed in your session. Encourage them to keep the bookmark in their Bible or their *Embraced by God* participant book as a reminder that they are loved unconditionally by God.

## Embrace His Love (5 minutes; Extended Option 10-15 minutes)

Conclude the session with the music video "Come Thou Fount." Introduce the video by saying that God's unending blessings, favor, and love are like a flowing fountain that never ceases. Invite participants to bask in the fountain of God's love with humble hearts of gratitude and praise as they prayerfully meditate on the words of "Come Thou Fount" or join in singing along.

# Notes

Play the music video (5:00 minutes). Then pray this prayer or one of your own:

*Sweet heavenly Father,*

*We thank You for embracing us in your love today and for the way that You have moved in our hearts. Help us to accept Your unconditional love and discover that we matter so very much to You. Help us to set aside our negative self-talk and the ugly messages we have believed. As we learn to listen to Your voice, may we discover who and whose we are. We love You, Lord. In Jesus' name, we pray. Amen.*

### Extended Option

After showing the music video, invite the women to divide into small groups of three to four for a time of prayer. Ask them to share joys and concerns as well as highlights from their discoveries during the week and this session.

When the groups are finished praying together, close your time by reading aloud the following promises. Instruct the women to respond to each statement with the corresponding "I am…" response.

You are loved. (I am loved.)
You are treasured. (I am treasured.)
You are accepted. (I am accepted.)
You are redeemed. (I am redeemed.)
You are gifted. (I am gifted.)
You are unequalled. (I am unequalled.)
You are preferred. (I am preferred.)
You are favored. (I am favored.)
You are God's favorite. (I am God's favorite.)
You are blessed. (I am blessed.)

Amen!

# Week 2

# YOU ARE BEAUTIFUL TO GOD

## Leader Preparation (Before the Session)

### Scripture Focus

*"The king is enthralled by your beauty; honor him, for he is your lord."*

Psalm 45:11 NIV

### Key Bible Story

This week, you read about three different nameless women who needed a life-changing encounter at just the right time in their lives. First, Jesus met up with the woman at Jacob's well. To begin with she had two strikes against her: she was female and she was a Samaritan. According to the custom of the day, Jesus had no business engaging in conversation with this woman. She had been with multiple men and was now living with a man who was not her husband. No one respected her or even saw her. *But Jesus saw her. He knew her. He knew what she needed to get from where she was to where she needed and longed to be.*

Then, there was the woman who had been caught in adultery. Some religious leaders had brought her to Jesus to try to trick Him into blasphemy. But Jesus turned the situation on them. He defused the focus on the woman by putting it on the same religious leaders who had been so quick to condemn the woman and confound Jesus. In front of all those people He leveled the playing field. He demonstrated that her sin was no more or less than the sin of anyone else standing ready to throw stones. In the eyes of the crowd gathered, this woman had no worth, no value. She was a pawn in this story. *But Jesus saw her. He knew her. He knew what she needed to get from where she was to where she needed and longed to be.*

Finally, there was the woman with the "issue of blood." This woman had tried everything she could try. Out of money, out of ideas, and out of support, she knew that Jesus was her last best shot at healing. I can imagine that she had to summon all of her remaining pride and courage to walk into that crowd of people, to force her way as close as she could to Jesus, just enough to touch His outer robe. And Jesus, though busy and in demand, knew that someone had touched Him. No one else around saw this woman crawl through the crowd of people, but when Jesus turned He saw this woman. *He knew her. He knew what she needed to get from where she was to where she needed and longed to be.*

# Notes

Jesus sees us. He knows us. No matter where we come from, what we've done, or what issue we are trapped in—He calls us beautiful. That is the gospel truth for us today.

**Objective**

Today you'll help the women in your group discover that when God looks upon each of them, He sees a beautiful masterpiece.

**What You Will Need**
- *Embraced by God* DVD and DVD player
- Index cards and pens (for Be About His Love Extended Option)

## Warm Up to His Love (10 minutes; Extended Option 15 minutes)

**Welcome Activity**

Welcome participants and take some time to revisit names and introductions, if necessary. Make sure any new ladies feel welcomed and invited into the discussion. Go around the room and ask each participant to name three things that come to mind when she hears the word *beautiful*.

***Extended Option***

Make a list on a marker board or flip chart by completing this statement: "In order to be beautiful in the eyes of the world, you must . . . " Ask participants to finish the sentence as you write their answers on the board. Explain that today you are going to discover that although the world may not call you beautiful, God surely does. In fact, God not only calls us beautiful; He calls us His masterpiece.

**Recite the Memory Verse**

Read John 17:23 aloud together. You may want to write it on a marker board or flip chart. Then erase selected words, or flip the chart to another copy of the verse that has missing words (suggested words to omit are underlined). Try reading the verse together again, this time filling in the blanks by memory.

*"I will be in them and you will be in me so that they will be completely one. Then the world will know that you sent me and that you loved them just as much as you loved me."*
John 17:23 NCV

**Opening Prayer**

Pray this prayer or one of your own to begin your study today:

*Dear heavenly Father,*
*We confess that many times we feel so much less than beautiful. We feel torn down by the world, and we tear ourselves down too. It can be so easy to feel like no one sees us, knows us, or cares about what we have to offer. But You see us. You know us. And You call us beautiful when no one else does. You call us a masterpiece when*

Notes

*others see us as damaged goods. Thank you for seeing beauty in us. Thank you for knowing our name, for seeing us as individuals in a crowd, and for knowing exactly what we need in order to get where You want us to go. You are so very good to us. Speak into our time together the words that You would have us to hear. Draw us closer to You as we open our hearts, our ears, our eyes, and Your Word. We love you, Lord. We pray in Jesus' name. Amen.*

## Weekly Reading Recap

- You are validated. No matter what anyone has said or will say about you, in God's eyes you are seen, known, loved, and worthy to be called beautiful.
- When God calls us to share the Living Water with those around us who need it, He will equip us for the task.
- You are vindicated. No matter what you might have done in the past, even if you think it is unforgivable, God forgives. He wipes the slate clean for a fresh start.
- You are valued. No matter how low you feel or how insignificant you think your life may be, God sees a priceless treasure when He looks at you.
- You are never alone. In your joy and your grief, in your pain and your shame, God is there with you. Nothing can separate you from God's love.

# Bask in His Love (15-20 minutes)

Play the Week 2 video segment on the DVD. Invite participants to complete the Video Viewer Guide for Week 2 in the participant book as they watch.

# Talk About His Love (20 minutes; Extended Option 30 minutes)

## Discussion Points

1. Sometimes in our lives we get stuck "looking for love in all the wrong places" and come up empty. Our world is suffering from a love deficiency, but true love can only be found in one person, Jesus Christ. Love is not a warm and fuzzy feeling. Love is not an emotional urge or even a deep desire. Love is not feeling good about yourself or someone else. Love is not a sexual drive. Love is a person. That person is Jesus.
   - Where have you looked for love, approval, affirmation, or validation—in the past and in the present? What have been the results of that search?
   - Why is it so hard for us to remember that Jesus is the One to whom we should run when we need love, approval, and validation? What often keeps us from running to Jesus first?
   - How does it help us to remember that love is a person (Jesus) and not just a feeling?

Notes

2. Only Jesus can fix whatever is broken in your life and quench your thirst. He offers all that He is for all that you are. And He invites you to share His living water with others.
   - **Are you desperate for love?** What does Jeremiah 31:3 tell us is the answer to the need for love? (See Day 2.)
   - Has God ever given you a vision or burden to help hurting people? Is there a particular group of people you feel called to share God's love with?

3. Divide into three groups for Bible study. Assign each group one of the following Bible stories of Jesus' encounters with unnamed women: Group 1: John 4:1-42 (The Woman at the Well); Group 2: John 8:2-11 (The Woman Caught in Adultery); Group 3: Luke 8:40-48 (The Woman with the Issue of Blood). Ask the groups to read their passage and prepare to share the details of the story with the large group. After each small group has shared, discuss the following questions:
   - What do these passages tell us about who matters to God?
   - How do these stories demonstrate to us that God sees beauty and value where the world sees unwanted, unvalued garbage?
   - Do you see yourself in any of these women? How?
   - When have you experienced the validation, vindication, and valuation of God in powerful, life-changing ways in your life?

4. Jesus is never on a search-and-destroy mission as it concerns the Father's most-prized creations. He is interested in saving people from their sins, not punishing them for their sins. Jesus is always on a seek-to-save mission for lost and hurting souls.
   - Have you ever struggled to understand Jesus' mission to save us from our sins instead of punishing us for them? Explain.
   - The woman at the well could not argue that she had the best track record with men, and the woman caught in adultery was most-likely guilty. She may have been a pawn in a plot against Jesus, but she was guilty of the crime. How does the fact that Jesus knows our guilt and does not condemn us but lovingly calls us to repentance and restoration lead you to a deeper faith in Him?

5. It has been said that almost 90 percent of what women do is driven by guilt. You may have made some mistakes that have caused you pain and affected those you love. Now you are wracked with guilt. But hear this: Jesus loves you more than you know; you never again have to be consumed or controlled by guilt.
   - What kinds of things cause you to feel guilty?
   - How does guilt affect your daily life?
   - What would it take for you to believe Jesus' words "Neither do I condemn thee" as though He spoke them directly to you?
   - Why is it difficult sometimes to "give all your worries and cares to God" (1 Peter 5:7)?

Notes

6. Jesus is the absolute best at doing what He does: restoring broken lives. He masterfully heals wounded hearts, bruised bodies, and troubled minds. He perfectly restores dysfunctional families, broken fellowships, and dashed dreams.
   • Like the woman with the issue of blood, **what "issues" in your life have made you retreat from the world? How do these "issues" cause you to run to Jesus?** (See Day 4.)
   • When was the last time you experienced God's healing flow into your life, overcoming the pain you've carried?
   • How does the enemy convince you that your problems don't matter to God?
   • What do you know about what God thinks of you?

7. Jesus understands exactly how you feel. He understands how the world can assault you right down to the core and leave you standing alone, feeling isolated and vulnerable. He knows what concerns you during the day and what keeps you up late at night. Jesus understands you better than you understand yourself.
   • How does Jesus understand how we feel?
   • Why is important for us to remember that Jesus walked the earth, experienced fear and sadness and every other emotion, and knows the depth of concerns that trouble us?
   • How does knowing that Jesus understands you better than you understand yourself give you hope?

8. If you feel that life has cheated you out of a relationship or robbed you of your dignity, you are not alone. Look to Jesus as the answer to your problem. If satan has sold you a bill of goods and, in exchange, has tried to steal your joy, then you are not standing by yourself. Run, don't walk, to Jesus. He is your first choice, not your last resort.
   • When has Jesus been your last resort instead of your first choice?
   • What might have been different if you had run to Jesus first?
   • When have you experienced the joy and encouragement of running into the waiting arms of Jesus?

9. Take some time to read God's promises. Assign the following passages to volunteers (some may need to read more than one passage if your group is small): John 14:13-14; Jeremiah 31:3; Ephesians 1:6b; Psalm 45:11; Proverbs 18:24; John 6:35a; John 6:35b; John 6:37; 1 John 1:9; John 8:11; John 3:17; Luke 19:10; Jeremiah 31:34b; John 14:18; 1 Peter 5:7; 2 Corinthians 12:9; 1 Peter 1:17. Discuss what each verse teaches us about God's view of His beloved children.
   • When we feel guilty, underappreciated, out of ideas, and far from God, how can these promises point us back to the arms of Jesus?
   • You are beautiful to God. Name some words that come to mind when you consider that God looks upon you and sees His beautiful masterpiece.

# Notes

## Be About His Love (5 minutes; Extended Option 10 minutes)

Ask everyone to turn to a neighbor to talk about a particular challenge from the Be About His Love section of the weekly readings. Say something like this: *On Day 2 you read about Babbie's friend Lisa who had a burden to create opportunities for women to fellowship, sing, share stories, and pray together. Spend a few minutes dreaming about what that might look like in your church and/or community. Who could you work with, where might you host gatherings, and how would you get the word out?*

### *Extended Option*

Hand out index cards and pens. Ask participants to write down the baggage that keeps them from fully accepting that they are beautiful in God's eyes. This may be messages from others, negative self-talk, sins of the past, or other barriers to acceptance. Invite them to spend a moment in silent prayer, surrendering all of the baggage and asking God to take it from them. Encourage them to ask God for freedom from guilt and sin that keeps them from living the beautiful life that God has for them. When they are finished praying, tell them to tear up their cards and throw the scraps into the garbage. Declare that their baggage is lifted and they are free to run into the open arms of God.

## Embrace His Love (5 minutes; Extended Option 10-15 minutes)

Conclude the session with the music video "You Love Me." Invite the women to affirm the amazing love relationship we can have with God as they prayerfully listen to the words.

Play the music video (4:38 minutes). Then pray this prayer or one of your own:

*Sweet heavenly Father,*

*We thank You for embracing us in your love today and for the way that You have moved in our hearts. Help us to know and believe that You consider us beautiful—even when we may not feel like it. When we are critical of ourselves, remind us that You call us a masterpiece. Thank You for Your promise to be with us always and to love us with an everlasting love. Help us to believe. In Jesus' name, we pray. Amen.*

### *Extended Option*

After showing the music video, invite the women to divide into small groups of three to four for a time of prayer. Ask them to share joys and concerns as well as highlights from their discoveries during the week and this session.

When the groups are finished praying, close your time by having each woman turn to her neighbor and declare, "Everything God made is beautiful—including me."

# Week 3

# YOU ARE NEVER ALONE

## Leader Preparation (Before the Session)

### Scripture Focus

*"Lo, I am with you always, even unto the end of the world."*
Matthew 28:20 NKJV

### Key Bible Story

When the resurrected Jesus gathered His followers for the last time before He ascended to heaven, He gave them a promise that extends to us and encourages us as we follow Him in the world today. Jesus gave them what is known as The Great Commission, calling them to go into all the world and make disciples. Jesus had been with them teaching, comforting, and healing, and now they would carry on that work. The task may have seemed too great or overwhelming, but Jesus promised to be with them. In fact, He promised to be with them until the end of the present age.

Jesus promises to be with us—in our work, in our efforts to carry out His mission, in our joys, in our hopes, in our sorrow and pain, in our dreams, in our loneliness, and in our relationships. The One who is well acquainted with grief, fear, and pain is with us. He knows exactly what we need when we need it, and His presence is always with us.

### Objective

Today you'll help your group discover that walking with God means you are never, ever alone.

### What You Will Need

- *Embraced by God* DVD and DVD player

## Warm Up to His Love (10 minutes; Extended Option 15 minutes)

### Welcome Activity

Welcome participants and take some time to revisit names and introductions, if necessary. Make sure any new ladies feel welcomed and invited into the discussion. Ask participants what they think the difference is between being alone and being lonely. List their answers on a marker board or flip chart.

# Notes

### *Extended Option*

Spend a few minutes discussing how the hurried pace of daily life inhibits deep relationships and connectedness, which can lead to a feeling of loneliness.

### Recite the Memory Verse

Read John 17:23 aloud together. You may want to write it on a marker board or flip chart. Then erase selected words, or flip the chart to another copy of the verse that has missing words (suggested words to omit are underlined). Try reading the verse together again, this time filling in the blanks by memory.

> *"I will be <u>in them</u> and <u>you will be in me</u> so that they will be <u>completely one</u>. Then the world will know that you sent me and that you loved them just as much <u>as you loved me</u>."*
> John 17:23 NCV

### Opening Prayer

Pray this prayer or one of your own to begin your study today:

*Dear heavenly Father,*

*Loneliness can come in like a plague in our lives and make us think that we are all alone, that there is no one we can turn to. But we know, sweet Father, that You have promised to be with us always. You have promised to never leave us or forsake us. You have promised to be an ever-present help in our time of need. So, Lord, forgive us for having a pity party and getting stuck in our ruts. Help us to be in constant relationship with You so that we always know that You are present with us and we are never, ever truly alone. Come and illuminate Your Word today and open our hearts to receive Your instruction. We pray in Jesus' name. Amen.*

### Weekly Reading Recap

- God is near. There is nowhere you can go where God is not.
- God made you for relationship with Him. You can see Him everywhere you look—if you have eyes to see.
- God hears you when you call and loves to give good gifts to His children.
- Prayer is how we stay connected to God, and we have to train ourselves to live a life of prayer.
- God cares deeply about what matters to you and wants you to bring your cares and requests to Him first.

## Bask in His Love (15-20 minutes)

Play the Week 3 video segment on the DVD. Invite participants to complete the Video Viewer Guide for Week 3 in the participant book as they watch.

# Talk About His Love (20 minutes; Extended Option 30 minutes)

## Notes

**Discussion Points**

1. God created us to enjoy good relationships: first with Him and also with others.
   - What impact do great relationships have in your life?
   - Why do you think relationships are so important to God?
   - How can social media give us the illusion of being in relationship with lots of people? What does it mean to truly be in relationship with someone?
   - How would you describe a good relationship?

2. Life is richer because of relationships, but our hurried lifestyles often mean we have less time to invest in them. When we run ourselves ragged, we sap our physical strength to the degree that it robs us of the joy and meaning Jesus intended for our lives. Also, running at break-neck speed without slowing down to enjoy the relationships God has given you gives the enemy an opportunity to use your busyness against you.
   - What relationships cause your life to feel richer?
   - How does the hurried pace of life prevent real, life-giving connection with others?
   - How can the enemy use our busyness against us when it comes to relationships?
   - When have your relationships suffered because of your busy schedule?
   - How can we make space and time in our schedules for building and nurturing relationships—both with others and with God?

3. Being alone and being lonely are two different things. In recent years there has been a growing sense of loneliness and isolation largely due to advances in technology and busier lifestyles. Most people admit to being lonely at one time or another. Many reveal they have no one with whom they can share their feelings, so they turn to the Internet, drugs, or alcohol to dull the pangs of loneliness.
   - Have you experienced or witnessed a struggle with loneliness? What happened?
   - What are some other ways that we try to make up for the lonely feelings we might have?
   - Where should we turn when we feel the pangs of loneliness come on? What does Jeremiah 33:3 tell us to do? What does it promise us?

4. God is the only source of real love; He is the one cure for the pervasive feeling of loneliness. Whenever you feel empty inside, you can have sweet fellowship with Him.
   - When have you known a "sweet fellowship" with God at just the right time?
   - How have you experienced God expressing His love toward you?
   - How would you explain to someone else that God is the only cure for pervasive loneliness?

Notes

5. To see God in all of His glory, you don't have to look very far. Just look around at what is right in front of you. Look beyond your immediate view. Look upward to see the majesty of the open sky. Look inward and recognize that Christ is in you. Pay attention. Look for each opportunity to see our heavenly Father in this earthly realm. God, in all of His glory, longs to show how great He is in you.

- Where do you see God when you go about your day? **Where do you see God at work?** (See Day 1.)
- How does keeping our eyes open to God help us deal with feelings of loneliness?
- In what ways is God's presence always with us—even when we feel abandoned by our closest friends and loved ones? How have you experienced this in your own life?
- Have you ever thought that you were a burden to God or that your needs were not worth bringing to God? Why do you think you had these feelings?
- What does it mean to you that God longs to show you His glory and for you to come to Him with everything that weighs you down and brings you joy?
- **What is your hope in today?** (See Day 2.)

6. God wants to have an ongoing, loving, and life-giving conversation with you.
- What does an ongoing conversation with God look like?
- What does a loving relationship with God look like?
- What does a life-giving conversation with God look like?
- How do you start this kind of conversation with God?
- What does it take to keep the conversation going?

7. Sometimes your situation can look pretty bleak. Your options can seem slim to none, and your resources may have dried up. But never give up on God or count Him out. Always allow Him to have the last word concerning your circumstances. God never gives up on you. He cares for you so much that He will provide a safe haven, a safe place, for you to rest when challenges are wearing you down.
- Has it ever seemed that your options were slim and your resources were few? **When have you felt like you were out of everything—like you only had enough (fill-in-the-blank) to make it through one more moment?** (See Day 5.)
- What situations are weighing heavy on you right now?
- What is it like to experience God's safe place when challenges have worn you down? When have you had this experience of God's love and care?
- How does the promise of God's presence and nearness help you face challenges?

8. Divide into four groups for Bible study. Assign the following passages to each group:

# Notes

Group 1: Matthew 28:20; 1 Samuel 12:22; 2 Corinthians 1:3; 1 Timothy 6:17; Psalm 118:24; Colossians 1:27; Psalm 19:1

Group 2: 2 Peter 3:9; Jeremiah 3:33; Matthew 7:11; Psalm 17:6; Psalm 91:14-16; Psalm 4:1; John 16:13a; Philippians 4:6-7

Group 3: Psalm 55:22; Psalm 61:1-3; John 14:18; Philippians 4:19; Zephaniah 3:17; 2 Thessalonians 3:3; Isaiah 58:11; Psalm 27:14

Group 4: 1 Kings 17:8-16

Ask the groups to read their assigned verses and discuss what the passages teach us about God's promise to be with us.

- How do these promises encourage and instruct us about the character of God?
- What does it mean to you to know that God cares about you?
- How do these promises deepen our love walk with the Lord?

## Be About His Love (5 minutes; Extended Option 10 minutes)

Ask everyone to turn to a neighbor to talk about a particular challenge from the Be About His Love section of the weekly readings. Say something like this: *On Day 5 you made a list of concerns called My Cares and a second list named God Cares. How did it feel to write down your concerns and realize that God cares about every single thing on that list? Was it hard to accept that God cares about the littlest things and also the big things? Why or why not?*

### *Extended Option*
Sometimes spiritual friends can be a lifeline when we start to feel the pangs of loneliness or need to be pointed back to the loving embrace of God. Invite your group to make a covenant of support by joining together as prayer friends. You may want to do this by creating a private Facebook page for your group and encouraging participants to post words of encouragement as well as fears, frustrations, and prayer concerns. Or, your group may be close enough to assign partners who will check in on each other or be that first phone call when feelings of loneliness and defeat arise.

## Embrace His Love (5 minutes; Extended Option 10-15 minutes)

Conclude the session with the music video "I Love You, I Do." Introduce the video by telling the women that this is a love song from the heart of God to each of us. Tell each woman to listen as if God were actually singing the words directly to her, because this is how God truly feels about her.

Play the music video (4:49 minutes). Then pray this prayer or one of your own:

# Notes

*Sweet heavenly Father,*

*We thank You for embracing us in Your love today and for the way that You have moved in our hearts. Help us to remember that we are never, ever alone in this world. You are always with us. Lord, help us to fight loneliness by spending time with You in prayer and in Your Word. As we gather as sisters, help us to urge and encourage one another to lean into You when we need companionship. Thank You for Your great and incomparable love. In Jesus' name, we pray. Amen.*

## Extended Option

After showing the music video, invite the women to divide into small groups of three to four for a time of prayer. Ask them to share joys and concerns as well as highlights from their discoveries during the week and this session.

When the groups are finished praying together, close your time by inviting the women to offer one another an embrace—not a casual pat on the back but a heartfelt embrace. As they do, ecourage them to recite this benediction from Numbers 6:24: "The Lord bless you and keep you" (NIV).

# Week 4

# YOU HAVE EVERYTHING
# YOU NEED IN GOD

## Leader Preparation (Before the Session)

### Scripture Focus

*"Are you tired? Worn out? Burned out on religion? Come to me. Get away with me and you'll recover your life. I'll show you how to take a real rest. Walk with me and work with me—watch how I do it. Learn the unforced rhythms of grace. I won't lay anything heavy or ill-fitting on you. Keep company with me and you'll learn to live freely and lightly.*

Matthew 11:28-30 *THE MESSAGE*

### Key Bible Story

Throughout His earthly life, Jesus continually pointed His followers to His Father's loving care and provision. He announced that His way of life is not like our hurry and worry lifestyle. No, His offer is a life of rest, peace, and assurance. His way is not burdensome and full of drama. No, His ways are good and lovely and wonderful.

In Matthew 11:28-30 Jesus invites us into a whole other way of life—another-worldly life, the way of lightness and freedom. Jesus proves that He is the only One who knows the Father and that He is the One through whom we have access to real, good, fruitful, and abundant life.

### Objective

Today you'll help your group discover that God meets all their needs according to His glorious riches in Christ Jesus.

### What You Will Need

- *Embraced by God* DVD and DVD player
- Small bottles of water, one for each participant (for Embrace His Love Extended Option)

## Warm Up to His Love (10 minutes; Extended Option 15 minutes)

### Welcome Activity

Welcome participants and ask each woman to turn to her neighbor and share a time when she had to place her trust in another person or in God. Talk for a few minutes about how easy or difficult it is to determine that it is safe to trust someone.

Notes

### *Extended Option*

Make a list of all of the things that women worry about, from the littlest stressors to the major life decisions to the scenarios we make up just to have something to worry about. Talk about why we worry and the reality that our worry exposes a lack of trust in God.

### Recite the Memory Verse

Read John 17:23 aloud together. You may want to write it on a marker board or flip chart. Then erase selected words, or flip the chart to another copy of the verse that has missing words (suggested words to omit are underlined). Try reading the verse together again, this time filling in the blanks by memory.

*"I will be in them and you will be in me so that they will be completely one. Then the world will know that you sent me and that you loved them just as much as you loved me."*
John 17:23 NCV

### Opening Prayer

Pray this prayer or one of your own to begin your study today:

*Dear heavenly Father,*

*You are so generous, loving, and trustworthy. You are kind, compassionate, and ever-present. You are awesome, wonderful, and truly amazing. We confess that even though we know these things about You, we still worry about so many things. But Lord, You have invited us to come to You and find rest. And so today, sweet Father, we come before You and lay our worries at Your feet. We want to seek You first and trust Your loving care. Give us faith, dear Lord, to know and to remember that You have promised to supply our needs and that Your provision is immeasurable. In Jesus' precious name we pray. Amen.*

### Weekly Reading Recap

- God is trustworthy. We don't need to be afraid to jump right into His arms.
- God's wisdom is perfect. When we don't understand the why of our circumstances, we can trust that God is good and He works all things together for good.
- God gives us courage to face our circumstances with boldness. We may not know why God leads us the way He does, but we can be sure that He will give us the courage to accomplish His purposes.
- God gives us confidence to face our trials and battles with the assurance of victory because we know that He is on our side.
- God invites us to rest from our weariness, to set down the cares of this life and trust Him to lead us, guide us, and show us His way of living.

## Bask in His Love (15-20 minutes)

Play the Week 4 video segment on the DVD. Invite participants to complete the Video Viewer Guide for Week 4 in the participant book as they watch.

## Talk About His Love (20 minutes; Extended Option 30 minutes)

# Notes

**Discussion Points**

1. The Lord Jesus is the only One who is truly worthy of complete trust. He provides full confidence for all of your uncertainties. He is sure, reliable, proved, consistent, and dependable. God watches over us in a very personal way, reassuring us time and again that He is on our side.

   • Remember from Day 1 in your readings this week the story about learning to swim in the deep end of the pool. Have you jumped into the "deep end" in your relationship with God—into a trust-God-with-all-your-heart type of relationship? If so, describe what this is like. If not, what is holding you back?

   • When have you experienced apprehension about trusting God with a situation or concern?

   • Why is it often difficult to put our complete and total trust in God? **How can you trust God and jump headlong into the safety of God's outstretched arms? What would this mean for you?** (See Day 1.)

2. Ask a volunteer to read aloud Proverbs 3:5-6. What does this passage teach us about God's ways?

   • When have you leaned on your own understanding and fell flat on your face?

   • What does it mean to acknowledge God in all your ways?

   • How has God proven to you that when you seek Him and trust Him, He makes your path straight?

   • How have your spiritual friends helped you lean on God's understanding?

3. God is all-knowing, omniscient. He understands everything there is to know about time and space because He created them. He knows about the past, the present, and the future—because He lives in the eternal realm outside the sphere of time and seasons. Our heavenly Father has complete knowledge and understanding about people, as well as powers in the spiritual realm. He created it all. His understanding is perfect.

   • If God knows every little detail about our lives and has promised to take care of us, why do we sometimes lack confidence that God will do what He says He will do?

   • What can we do to gain confidence or determine to be confident in God's immeasurable provision?

   • Read Psalm 111:7-8. **What do these verses say about God's wisdom?** (See Day 2.)

4. Ask some volunteers to read aloud the following scriptures: Proverbs 30:5; Proverbs 3:5-6; Matthew 6:9-13; 2 Samuel 22:31-32; James 1:5; 2 Corinthians 4:18.

   • Think about what you just heard. Declare some statements about God that you know to be true based on these Scriptures.

   • Why is it so hard to trust what we can't see?

# Notes

5. Trusting God is an all-or-nothing endeavor. It's kind of like being pregnant. You either are pregnant or you're not. There's no in between. Likewise, you either trust God, or you don't. To walk by faith, you must decide whether you will trust Him and be at peace or worry and stress over every situation.
   - How is trusting God an all-or-nothing endeavor?
   - What situation do you face now that requires you to trust God?

6. Jesus reminded the crowds not to worry. God is all-knowing, all-loving, and so very trustworthy. He is all wisdom and has every answer for every problem we will ever face. We can trust His loving hand to guide us.
   - **Why do we worry so? What things can you add to your life by worrying?** (See Day 2.)
   - Have someone read aloud Matthew 6:31-34. What does Jesus say about God's loving provision in our lives?
   - How can trust in God's provision help us put worry out of our hearts?

7. Sometimes our worry seems warranted. We do OK to resist worry about the day-to-day matters. But sometimes we face battles in this life against disease, financial security, relationships in distress, spiritual warfare, and so much more. We worry about having the strength to make it to the other side of those trials. The promise is that God has given you courage to go to battle in His name, knowing He has already provided everything you need for victory.
   - How can we trust God to meet our needs even in the most grave of circumstances?
   - What does it mean to take courage in God? **What situations in your life require courage on your part?** (See Day 3.)

8. Surely if anyone could worry about facing a battle, it would be Joshua. Under the Lord's direction, Joshua would take God's people into a great, new land. To carry out God's plan, they would have to conquer the inhabitants of this land of promise: Canaan. That meant, first of all, overtaking the great and mighty city of Jericho. Ask some volunteers to read the following excerpts from Joshua's story: Joshua 1:1-12; 6:1-5; 6:6-14; 6:15-21.
   - What do you think the people thought when they heard Joshua's plan was to simply march around the city?
   - What happened because Joshua trusted God's ways, even though they might have seemed slow or unconventional?
   - When has God's plan for your life felt slow or unconventional?
   - How did God bring about victory at just the right time?
   - **What does it look like for you to be confident in the promises of God?** (See Day 4.)

9. Do you know someone who is constantly on the run? From the moment she puts her feet on the floor at the crack of "dark-thirty" to the moment she lays her head down well after midnight, she's on the run—to work, to school, to the bank, to the cleaners, to the ball field, and to church. And of course, she runs behind. She

Notes

runs late. She runs out. She runs scared. The chaos hardly ever ceases. Even when she should be asleep, she lies awake with a long list of things to do and places to go running through her head. Now, she's running short on sleep! There's no rest for the weary, is there? Ah, but there is, my friend. Jesus personally invites you to step out of the fast lane.

- Does this woman seem familiar to you? In what ways?
- What happens to us when we are constantly on the run, worrying about getting here and there, worrying about the big and little things, just keeping on the move because we think the faster we go, the more in control we are?
- Read Matthew 11:28-30. What do you hear in Jesus' invitation? **Where does this extravagant, unconditional love and invitation to rest meet you today?** (See Day 5.)

## Be About His Love (5 minutes; Extended Option 10 minutes)

Ask everyone to turn to a neighbor to talk about a particular challenge from the Be About His Love section of the weekly readings. Say something like this: *On Day 2 you were challenged to write down your worries as they crept into your mind all day long. Then, you were to wad the paper up and throw them away. Did this tangible act of tossing your worries help you let go of worry? What was that experience like?*

### Extended Option

Write Matthew 11:28-30 from the *THE MESSAGE* on a marker board or flip chart. Ask them to turn to their neighbors and go line by line through the passage, discussing what makes them tired, worn out, and burned out. Ask them to discuss the life that Jesus describes and what it would be like to learn the "unforced rhythms of grace" and live "freely and lightly."

## Embrace His Love (5 minutes; Extended Option 10-15 minutes)

Conclude the session with the music video "I Believe." Introduce the video by saying that remembering and affirming who God is and what He has done for us helps to build our faith in God's provision and to give us the courage we need to face every circumstance. Invite the women to join in singing as they are comfortable, raising their voices loudly as they sing the words "I believe in you, Jesus."

Play the music video (4:00 minutes). Then pray this prayer or one of your own:

*Sweet heavenly Father,*

*We thank You for embracing us in Your love today and for the way that You have moved in our hearts. God, we confess that we are worriers. We confess that when Your time and ways confound us, we take matters into our own hands. Sweet heavenly Father, You have promised to be faithful and meet all of our needs. Lord, help us to*

# Notes

boldly and confidently trust Your ways and Your wisdom. We love You, Lord. In Jesus' name. Amen.

### Extended Option

After showing the music video, invite the women to divide into small groups of three to four for a time of prayer. Ask them to share joys and concerns as well as highlights from their discoveries during the week and this session.

When the groups are finished praying together, close your time by handing out small bottles of water to everyone. Tell participants that you are going to read aloud a few Scriptures as they feel the water give life and refreshment to their bodies. Invite them to drink the water as you read the Scripture verses.

*"All of you who are thirsty, come to the water! Whoever has no money, come, buy food and eat! Without money, at no cost, buy wine and milk."* (Isaiah 55:1 CEB)

*"Come! And let the one who is thirsty come! Let the one who wishes receive life-giving water as a gift."* (Revelation 22:17 CEB)

*"Everyone who drinks this water will be thirsty again, but whoever drinks from the water I give will never be thirsty again. The water that I give will become in those who drink it a spring of water that bubbles up into eternal life."* (John 4: 13-14 CEB)

# Week 5

# YOU HAVE A
# GOD-GIVEN PURPOSE

## Leader Preparation (Before the Session)

### Scripture Focus

*"So here's what I want you to do, God helping you: Take your everyday, ordinary life—your sleeping, eating, going-to-work, and walking-around life—and place it before God as an offering. Embracing what God does for you is the best thing you can do for him. Don't become so well-adjusted to your culture that you fit into it without even thinking. Instead, fix your attention on God. You'll be changed from the inside out. Readily recognize what he wants from you, and quickly respond to it. Unlike the culture around you, always dragging you down to its level of immaturity, God brings the best out of you, develops well-formed maturity in you.*

Romans 12:1-2 *THE MESSAGE*

### Key Bible Story

In Romans 12, Paul writes to the Roman church to urge them to give their whole lives to God as a sacrifice, to be used in whatever way God ordains. He uses the words "living sacrifice" to suggest that as we live and give ourselves to Christ, the very acts of our bodies and words of our mouths, the very breaths we take can be worship.

This is a call to surrender—to surrender hopes, dreams, control. In order to grow into spiritual maturity and see the fullness of what God created us to be, we have to lay ourselves down on the altar of God. We have to give ourselves completely to the work that God has to do in and through us. The world may try to tell us who we are and what we should be about, but Paul reminds us that the world has no power over us. The world does not define us or have the power to transform us. Only God can transform us into the likeness of Christ. Only Christ can empower us to accomplish that which God has called us to.

### Objective

Today you'll help your group discover that God has a specific plan and purpose for each of them.

### What You Will Need
- *Embraced by God* DVD and DVD player
- computers, notebooks, or tablets—or copies of a written spiritual gifts assessment (for Embrace His Love Extended Option)

33

# Notes

## Warm Up to His Love (10 minutes; Extended Option 15 minutes)

### Welcome Activity

Welcome participants. Go around the room and have each participant finish this sentence: When I was a child I wanted to grow up to be a _____.

### *Extended Option*

Have the women turn to their neighbors to discuss the difference between what they thought they would do as a child and what they are doing now. Did they follow and realize that dream? Did they choose something else? Are they still searching for what they were made to do?

### Recite the Memory Verse

Read John 17:23 aloud together. You may want to write it on a marker board or flip chart. Then erase selected words, or flip the chart to another copy of the verse that has missing words (suggested words to omit are underlined). Try reading the verse together again, this time filling in the blanks by memory.

> *"I will be in them and you will be in me so that they will be completely one. Then the world will know that you sent me and that you loved them just as much as you loved me."*
>
> John 17:23 NCV

### Opening Prayer

Pray this prayer or one of your own to begin your study today:

*Sweet heavenly Father,*

*You have searched us and You know us. You knit us together. You ordained all our days. You know the plans You have for us. We praise You for we are fearfully and wonderfully made. Thank You for Your great love, for Your tender mercies, for Your amazing grace, and for Your mighty work in our lives. Thank You for knowing us, for loving us, and for calling us to a specific purpose in this world. God, reveal to us Your plan and purpose. Illuminate Your Word in our lives so that we can't miss it. Bind us together as a sisterhood to encourage one other and cheer one another on to live out our God-given purposes. We give You all the praise and glory. In Jesus' name we pray. Amen.*

### Weekly Reading Recap

- You are custom-designed: fearlessly and wonderfully created on purpose to fulfill a divine, God-given purpose.
- You were created to praise and extol your Creator, Father God.
- God is for you, not against you. There isn't a single adverse situation in your life that God can't use to bring about greatness in you.

- In Christ, you have everything you need to accomplish His perfect plan and purpose for Your life.
- As long as You have life, the very breath of God within you, there is always hope for you.

## Bask in His Love (15-20 minutes)

Play the Week 5 video segment on the DVD. Invite participants to complete the Video Viewer Guide for Week 5 in the participant book as they watch.

## Talk About His Love (20 minutes; Extended Option 30 minutes)

**Discussion Points**

1. Ask volunteers to read aloud Jeremiah 29:11 and Psalm 139:15-16.
   - What do these verses tell us about God's plans for us?
   - How do these promises give us a sense of security?
   - **What would change in your life if you looked first to Jesus for your purpose and identity?** (See Day 1.)
   - What does a prosperous and hopeful future look like to you?

2. God created you because He wanted to have a close, meaningful relationship with you. Your primary purpose is to give God first place in your life and make Him your main priority. Discovering God's plan for you begins with returning His embrace: finding Him and putting Him first. Read aloud Romans 12:1-2 and Matthew 10:39.
   - What do you think it means to be a living sacrifice?
   - What does it mean to be conformed to the world?
   - What does it mean to be transformed by the renewing of your mind?
   - What does Jesus mean by looking to Him to find yourself?

3. You are a distinctive expression of God's creativity in the earth. When God designed you, He placed within you certain gifts and abilities that are unique to who you are.
   - Instruct participants to take one minute and write down as many unique gifts and abilities they can think of that God has placed in them—either in their books or on paper you provide.
   - Ask volunteers to share some of the gifts and abilities that they wrote down, and invite members of the group to affirm any gifts they also recognize in these persons.
   - How do you think these gifts and abilities help you live out God's purpose for your life?

Notes

4. God has given you gifts and abilities that come alive when you are in your element. As you flow in your God-given gifts and abilities, your genius is put on display. When you do what you were born to do, you shine like a star.
   - **What are you naturally good at? What do you love to do? What do people tell you that you have a gift for?** (See Day 2.)
   - When have you felt like you were doing the thing you were created to do?
   - When have you felt in your element and shining like a star?
   - In what ways is doing the thing you were born to do an act of worship? Is it possible for *everything* you do to become an act of worship? If so, how?

5. Our culture measures success by accomplishments, awards, and applause. But according to God's Word, success isn't wrapped up in possessions, fame, or recognition. Success is not determined by who you are; it is determined by who you are with.
   - How would you define a life of success?
   - How does the world define success?
   - How does God define success for you?

6. Ask volunteers to read the story of David's anointing in 1 Samuel 16:1-13.
   - How would you describe Jesse's other sons compared to David?
   - Why do you think Samuel assumed one of the sons there with him would be God's chosen?
   - **Why do you think Samuel wasn't interested in the other brothers [after seeing David]?** (See Day 3.)
   - What do you think David's brothers thought when Samuel announced that David was the one God had chosen?
   - What do you remember about how God worked in David's life from that moment on?

7. Regardless of your faults and foibles, God can and will use you to accomplish His purposes. Over and over again, God uses people with challenges and weaknesses to demonstrate His great strength. When you speak negatively about yourself, you defeat God's purpose in your life.
   - How easy or difficult is it to speak positively about the gifts God has placed in you?
   - Where do you think negative self-talk comes from?
   - How can we shut out the negative self-talk and have confidence in who God created us to be?
   - When have you had confidence and assurance that God was using you to accomplish His purposes?

8. Even when you don't see any evidence of God in a situation, you can have confident assurance that He's behind the scenes working all things together for your good. When everything seems to be going all wrong, God will cause your circumstances to work out all right.

- Recall the story of Joseph from your readings this week. How was God with Joseph, behind the scenes making all things work together for Joseph's good?
- When have you experienced God working behind the scenes in your life?
- Have volunteers read aloud the following passages: **Psalm 27:14; James 4:7; Galatians 6:7-10; Romans 5:1-5; Hebrews 6:17-20; Psalm 103:1-5; Psalm 42:11. What promises are found in these verses?** (See Day 5.)
- How can you live with confidence and assurance that God will accomplish His purpose in you whether you are in the pit or on the mountaintop?

## Be About His Love (5 minutes; Extended Option 10 minutes)

Ask everyone to turn to a neighbor to talk about a particular challenge from the Be About His Love section of the weekly readings. Say something like this: *On Day 2 you answered some questions about your gifts and abilities. Talk with your partner about what you discovered about the gifts and abilities God has placed in you and how you might use them to accomplish God's purpose in your life.*

### Extended Option

If you have access to the Internet in your meeting space, provide enough computers and/or tablets for members to complete an online spiritual gifts assessment at http://www.ministrymatters.com/spiritualgifts/. Or, obtain a written assessment with instructions for analyzing results and make copies for the group. After participants have received or determined their results, talk about any surprises or discoveries.

## Embrace His Love (5 minutes; Extended Option 10-15 minutes)

Conclude the session with the music video "Love Song." Introduce the video by saying that this song talks about living our lives as a love song to God in response to all He has done for us. Read the chorus aloud before playing the video:

> *Let my life be a love song to You*
> *Every cry be a love song to You*
> *Day and night be a love song to You*
> *To You, to You, to You**

# Notes

Play the music video (4:44 minutes). Then pray this prayer or one of your own:

*Sweet heavenly Father,*

*We thank You for embracing us in Your love today and for the way that You have moved in our hearts. Lord, we are so grateful that You have placed within us gifts and abilities that You designed just for us. We lay ourselves before You as a living sacrifice, giving ourselves wholly to You and to Your purpose in our lives. Thank You for the awesome work that You are planning to do in and through us. Help us to put away the negative self-talk that keeps us from believing that we are good enough or smart enough or beautiful enough to do the work to which You call us. Give us faith to believe that You are faithful to do exactly what You said You will do. We love You, Lord. We pray in Jesus' name. Amen.*

### Extended Option

After showing the music video, invite the women to divide into small groups of three to four for a time of prayer. Ask them to share joys and concerns as well as highlights from their discoveries during the week and this session.

When the groups are finished praying, read aloud Psalm 27:14 (below). Then instruct each woman to insert her name after every phrase as you read the verse aloud again, pausing after each phrase. Encourage them this week to find hope in the fact that God has called and equipped them to accomplish His great purposes in their lives.

*Wait on the LORD;*
*Be of good courage,*
*And He shall strengthen your*
*heart;*
*Wait, I say, on the LORD!*
Psalm 27:14 NKJV

# Week 6

# YOU CAN ACCOMPLISH GREAT THINGS IN GOD'S NAME

## Notes

## Leader Preparation (Before the Session)

### Scripture Focus

*"Lord, if it is You, command me to come to You on the water."*

Matthew 14:28b NKJV

### Key Bible Story

After Jesus had fed five thousand people with five loaves of bread and two fish, Jesus sent the crowds away and told the disciples to take the boat to the other side of the lake. Matthew tells us that Jesus went up to the mountain to pray. You can imagine that Jesus must have been tired from preaching and performing the miracle of feeding all of those people. Right after this scene, Jesus would go on to walk on water and heal masses of people. I love that Matthew shows us that even Jesus needed quiet time with His Father in the midst of all that God was doing in and through Him.

When Jesus comes down from His mountain-top prayer time, He approaches the boat that carried the disciples by walking on the water. Now, usually, this story gets told with a focus on Peter's doubt and subsequent sinking. But I want you to pay attention to the fact that Peter dared to get out of the boat in the first place. The other disciples sat afraid in the boat. Peter bravely asked Jesus to command him to get out there on the water and, what's more, he went! Sure, Peter was scared, with the angry waves dashing around him, but he will always be remembered as the disciple who walked on the water with Jesus. He accomplished an impossible feat, even during a moment of human doubt. This is surely a great lesson for us to learn as we navigate life's deep waters.

### Objective

Today you'll help your group discover that they can do amazing things when they step out of the boat with Jesus.

### What You Will Need

- *Embraced by God* DVD and DVD player
- Sheet of paper and a pen for each woman (Welcome Activity and Embrace His Love Extended Options)

# Notes

## Warm Up to His Love (10 minutes; Extended Option 15 minutes)

### Welcome Activity

Welcome participants. Go around the room and have each participant share a time when she took a leap of faith, telling what happened as a result of the leap. Or invite them to share their dreams and passions.

### *Extended Option*

Give each participant a sheet of paper and a pen. Ask them to write the words, "I dream . . ." at the top. Then, have them write a one-sentence dream that they have asked God to accomplish through them. When they are finished, go around the room and ask them to hold up their signs and share their dreams.

### Recite the Memory Verse

Read John 17:23 aloud together. You may want to write it on a marker board or flip chart. Then erase selected words, or flip the chart to another copy of the verse that has missing words (suggested words to omit are underlined). Try reading the verse together again, this time filling in the blanks by memory.

> *"I will be <u>in</u> <u>them</u> and <u>you</u> <u>will</u> <u>be</u> <u>in</u> <u>me</u> so that they will be <u>completely</u> <u>one</u>. Then <u>the</u> <u>world</u> <u>will</u> <u>know</u> that <u>you</u> <u>sent</u> <u>me</u> and that <u>you</u> <u>loved</u> <u>them</u> just as much <u>as</u> <u>you</u> <u>loved</u> <u>me</u>."*
>
> John 17:23 NCV

### Opening Prayer

Pray this prayer or one of your own to begin your study today:

*Dear heavenly Father,*

*We praise You right now for who You are and all You've done in our lives and in our time together. Thank You for revealing more and more of who You are. Thank You for Your wide-open arms waiting to enfold us in Your embrace. Thank You for a heart filled with faith, allowing us to accomplish great things. God, we want to walk on the water with You; give us the boldness, courage, and faith to get out of the boat right now. Call us out of our comfort zone and into the deep water with You. We love You, Lord. In Jesus' name we pray. Amen.*

### Weekly Reading Recap

- Our confidence comes not from who we are but from whose we are. When we know to whom we belong, we have courage to take a leap of faith.
- Every challenge can be a launching pad for success. There is always room to stage a comeback.
- We don't need to waste our time and energy with self-pity. Jesus turns our trials into testimonies.
- We can make a difference in this world. Jesus calls us to be the "salt of the earth."
- Love is our greatest tool to accomplish great things in this world.

# Notes

## Bask in His Love (15-20 minutes)

Play the Week 6 video segment on the DVD. Invite participants to complete the Video Viewer Guide for Week 6 in the participant book as they watch.

## Talk About His Love (20 minutes; Extended Option 30 minutes)

**Discussion Points**

1. Invite one or more volunteers to read aloud the story of Peter walking on water found in Matthew 14:22-33. (See Day 1.)
   • What does the passage say the disciples thought at first when they saw a man walking on the water?
   • **What did Jesus say in verse 27?**
   • **How did Peter respond to the man on the water (verse 28)?**
   • **What did Jesus say to Peter that got him out of the boat (verse 29)?**
   • **How did Jesus respond to Peter's plea (verse 31)?**
   • **What was the response of the group when Peter and Jesus were back in the boat (verses 32-33)?**

2. Peter is often looked down upon because fear gripped his heart and he began to sink. But while the others cowered in fear, Peter was the only disciple who dared to take a huge step of faith and get out of the boat.
   • Why do you think we tend to focus on Peter's doubt and sinking rather than on his courage to get out of the boat?
   • What do you think kept the other disciples in the boat?
   • What do you think you would have done if you had been in that boat?

3. If you are going to follow Jesus, at some point you will have to leave familiar surroundings and the comfort of the crowd. Your decision to take a risk may not always be popular. Others may try to discourage you and suggest that you take an easier way, but you will never grow in faith listening to the naysayers.
   • What do the naysayers say that convinces you it's better to stay safe inside your comfort zone?
   • How can we find the courage to be like Peter and step out of our "boats"?

4. Greatness lies deep within you. God has given you an assignment, and it's up to you to gain a clear understanding from Him of just what that assignment is. Once you have an understanding, pray for the faith, vision, wisdom, strength, and obedience to go and do it.
   • Take a minute to think about what your God-given assignment might be. What has God created you to do?
   • What does it look like for you to step out of the boat in your life?
   • What is keeping you from taking that leap of faith?
   • Or, if you have taken the leap of faith, what is your testimony of being out there in the deep end with Jesus?

# Notes

5. Ask volunteers to read aloud an excerpt of Paul and Barnabas's first missionary journey in Acts 13: 44–14:23. (See Day 2.)
   - **What was the work that Paul and Barnabas were called to do?**
   - **What were the obstacles they faced along the way?**
   - **How did Paul and Barnabas respond to the opposition?**
   - When have you felt knocked down or set back in your pursuits?
   - What helps you get back up and press on?

6. The first step after being knocked down is simply to get up. Don't wallow in the mire and throw a pity party. People don't want to come to pity parties. Don't put on the cloak of guilt. Don't become paralyzed by fear. Realize what's happening and look it square in the face. Self-pity, guilt, and fear are arrows that the enemy uses to wound your spirit and render you ineffective.
   - Why do you think we are so prone to throwing pity parties? Where do you think the pity comes from?
   - Where does guilt come from when we face setbacks?
   - What does it mean to look at a pity-party square in the face and say "no way"? Practically speaking, *how* can we do this?
   - When has the enemy sucked you into self-pity and feelings of guilt, fear, and ineffectiveness? How did you overcome those feelings?

7. Read aloud John 5:1-8. If we look closely at this story, we see the man's helplessness, self-pity, and blaming in the excuse he gives Jesus. Jesus challenges us to assume a measure of responsibility and exercise self-control, so we can master the circumstances that once mastered us.
   - How was the man by the pool having a pity party?
   - What did Jesus ask him? How did he respond to Jesus?
   - What simple words did Jesus speak to call the man out of his pity party?
   - When have you found yourself wallowing in pity instead of trusting Jesus to walk you to a place of healing and wholeness? **What excuses have prevented you from finding healing?** (See Day 3.)
   - How has God worked in your life through narrow escapes, economic hardships, the loss of loved ones, broken relationships, disappointments, or failure?
   - How did you find God to be faithful and big enough to accomplish His work in you, even in the time of trial?
   - How did you turn your trial into a testimony?

8. As believers in His name, Christ has assigned us the great task of adding love to this world's bitter mix. He has given us the mission of making the world a little bit more like heaven on earth—of making a big difference in the world.
   - What are some ways that we can add love to this world's bitter mix?
   - What does Jesus mean when He calls us the "salt of the earth" in Matthew 5:13?
   - What did you discover this week about what it means to bring Christ's love to the world? How can you accomplish great things by showing love?

# Notes

## Be About His Love (5 minutes; Extended Option 10 minutes)

Ask everyone to turn to a neighbor to talk about a particular challenge from the Be About His Love section of the weekly readings. Say something like this: *On Day 2 you were asked to consider a trial or situation in your life that you can turn into a testimony. Share with your neighbor the testimony you discovered you have to tell.*

### Extended Option

Have a discussion about the ministries of your church and how your group might be intentional about showing love in specific ways. How could your group bless your church with acts of love? How could your group lead the way for your church to show acts of love in your community? Brainstorm some ideas and pray that God would use your group to accomplish His purposes for your church and community.

## Embrace His Love (5 minutes; Extended Option 10-15 minutes)

Conclude the session with the music video "(This Is) My Prayer for You." Introduce the video by saying that this song is a prayer spoken on their behalf as well as a prayer they are to offer for their sisters in Christ. Invite them to prayerfully meditate on the words and sing along on the chorus.

Play the music video (3:46 minutes). Then pray this prayer or one of your own:

*Sweet heavenly Father,*

*We thank You for embracing us in Your love today and for moving in our hearts. Lord, You call us—command us—to get out of our boats and walk with You on the water. Help us to step out in faith and do amazing things in Your name. We ask You to accomplish amazing and wonderful things through us. We say yes, right here and now, to what You have in store for us. Thank You in advance for Your great and mighty work. In Jesus' name. Amen.*

### Extended Option

After showing the music video, invite the women to divide into small groups of three to four for a time of prayer. Ask them to share joys and concerns as well as highlights from their discoveries during the week and this session.

When the groups are finished praying, have participants hold up the signs they made earlier of their dreams. Ask participants to read their I Dream signs again and say out loud, "Lord, if it is You, command me to come to You on the water" (NKJV).

# Week 7

# YOU ARE EQUIPPED WITH UNIQUE GIFTS AND TALENTS

## Leader Preparation (Before the Session)

**Scripture Focus**

*Whatever you do, work at it with all your heart, as working for the Lord, not for men, since you know that you will receive an inheritance from the Lord as a reward. It is the Lord Christ you are serving.*

Colossians 3:23-24 NIV

**Key Bible Story**

Chapter 3 of Colossians is packed full of encouragement and instruction for a growing, thriving, love relationship with Jesus Christ. The chapter could be read as a practical guidebook for life with Christ. Verses 23-24 come at the end of a litany of instructions to clothe ourselves with kindness and compassion, to put on love, to forgive one another, to set aside anger and immorality, and to be thankful. This guide to Christ-like living is a response to the sacrifice that Christ made on our behalf. Since we have been raised with Christ—in other words, saved for and invited into His kingdom—we have a new outlook. Our minds focus on Christ and His way of life instead of the ways of this world.

As we learn to set our minds on Christ, turn our backs to sin, and take on the attributes of Jesus, Paul tells us that whatever we do, wherever we go, whomever we work for, whatever our task, we are called to work and act as if we are working with and for the Lord.

**Objective**

Today you'll help your group to discover that God has equipped them with unique gifts and talents, and that their task is to make themselves available to be used by God.

**What You Will Need**
- *Embraced by God* DVD and DVD player
- Sheet of paper and a pen for each participant (Welcome Activity Extended Option)

# Notes

## Warm Up to His Love (10 minutes; Extended Option 15 minutes)

**Welcome Activity**

Welcome participants. Go around the room and have each participant share a time when she felt completely available to do whatever God called her to do. Then, ask the women to briefly share some things that can make us unavailable for what God calls us to do, as well as ways we can be open for God to use us.

### *Extended Option*

Give each participant a sheet of paper and a pen. Remind them that over the last three weeks, they have focused on God's purpose for them, their ability to accomplish great things, and God's promise to equip them for whatever He calls them to do. Have them write the word *Purpose* at the top of the page, the word *Dreams* in the middle of the page, and the words *Equipped With* toward the bottom of the page.

Under the word *Purpose*, ask them to write what God has been saying to them about their purpose. Under the word *Dreams*, ask them to list the visions that God has placed in them of what He can accomplish in and through them. Finally, under the words *Equipped With*, ask them to list all of the gifts, talents, special abilities, and interests that God has placed in them. When they are finished, invite volunteers to share what they believe is their purpose, what God might be calling them to, and how God has equipped them for that task.

**Recite the Memory Verse**

By now you and your group are well on your way to committing to memory John 17:23 and hiding this beautiful truth deep in your hearts. Write the verse on a board or flip chart. Read aloud the entire passage and emphasize the words *"I will be in them and you will be in me,"* speaking that phrase a little louder than the rest of the passage. Then erase the board or flip the chart and recite the verse together from memory, again emphasizing the same phrase.

> *"**I will be in them and you will be in me** so that they will be completely one. Then the world will know that you sent me and that you loved them just as much as you loved me."*
> John 17:23 NCV

**Opening Prayer**

Pray this prayer or one of your own to begin your study today:

*Dear heavenly Father,*

*We are so thankful that You love to embrace us in Your loving arms. Lord, we thank You for creating us, calling us, and equipping us to do great things in this world. Reveal to us more and more about Your purpose for our lives. We make ourselves one-hundred percent available to You right now, in this very moment. We pray in Your name. Amen.*

**Weekly Reading Recap**

- When our view seems hopeless and there is no one to encourage us, we learn to encourage ourselves.
- We can encourage ourselves by looking back and looking around at all that God has done in our lives.

# Notes

- We can equip ourselves to be ready when God calls us by practicing a life of obedience.
- We equip ourselves to be ready when God calls us when we learn to depend on Him completely.
- We grow into the work that God calls us to when we envision ourselves growing and thriving as His disciples in this world.

## Bask in His Love (15-20 minutes)

Play the Week 7 video segment on the DVD. Invite participants to complete the Video Viewer Guide for Week 7 in the participant book as they watch.

## Talk About His Love (20 minutes; Extended Option 30 minutes)

**Discussion Points**
1. Do you have disappointments that weigh heavily in your heart? Have your hopes and dreams literally gone up in smoke? Are you feeling the deep pain and sting of suffering a great loss? Take comfort. You don't have to wait for others to speak the encouraging words you long to hear. You can speak over yourself like David did and encourage yourself in the Lord. Read aloud 1 Samuel 30:1-6.
   - Why did David have reason to be discouraged?
   - What words do you think came to David's mind when he began to encourage himself?
   - When have you faced devastation and discouragement? **When have you felt "pressed on every side" (NIV)?** (See Day 2.)
   - Where did you find encouragement?
   - What words from Scripture would you use to encourage yourself? (What psalms did you write in your book on Day 1?)

2. As God brings you to center stage, shining the spotlight on your gifts and abilities and using you to advance His kingdom, stay on the alert. Watch and pray because the enemy can recognize God's hand upon your life; he'll do whatever he can do to wound you and stall your progress.
   - When have you felt the enemy's attack on God's work in your life?
   - How can we keep the enemy from discouraging us?
   - When has God made a way for you to escape the enemy's attacks?

3. Ask a volunteer to read aloud Psalm 137. God has placed a harp deep within the human soul. This harp is an instrument of joy and worship that you can play no matter the circumstances.
   - When have you felt God's song in your heart, even when singing seemed like an absurd thing to do?
   - How can you sing God's song in your heart to encourage yourself when you feel defeated?

Notes

4. When life's circumstances keep you up all night and make you question God's purpose and your abilities to withstand the situation, remember the promises of God. Assign the following promises for volunteers to read aloud: **1 Peter 2:9; John 13:35; John 15:14; Isaiah 49:16; Matthew 5:13; Matthew 5:14; Romans 8:37; Numbers 13:30;** Psalm 1:1-2; Nehemiah 8:10 (see Day 2).
   • How do these promises remind us to be encouraged in the Lord?
   • What other verses come to mind when you remember the promises of God?
   • How has God been faithful to His promises in your life?

5. Recall the stories of Jochebed, Esther, and Mary, which you read on Day 3 of this week. These three women show us in different ways how God places us in certain situations and equips us to show His power and bring Him glory. These women obeyed God when they knew they had to do something.
   • What do these women teach us about the unique places and positions God puts us in order to accomplish His purpose?
   • What unique gifts and abilities did each of them have for her task?
   • How did obedience equip each woman to fulfill her mission? (See Day 3.)

6. Becoming who Christ has called us to be is our life's goal. We must take hold of His promises, hiding them within us, and then live them out in our daily lives. If you are doing anything less than your absolute best for the cause of Christ, it is mediocrity.
   • When have you experienced the joy of doing your absolute best for Christ?
   • What happens to our faith, our joy, and our lives when we fall into mediocrity?
   • What does it mean to do our absolute best as we live out the promise within us?

7. Divide into three groups and assign each group the following passage to read, and have them discuss how we can practice the instructions from this passage in our daily lives. Group 1: Colossians 3:23-24; Group 2: Ephesians 5:15-16; Group 3: Galatians 6:9. Then come back together as a large group and share, using the following questions.
   • What do these verses tell us about how to live with purpose?
   • How can we achieve this level of excellence in using our unique talents, gifts, and abilities?

8. We all want to be prosperous and successful in life. But sometimes we can do all the right things for all the wrong reasons. We can hold onto our stuff and miss Christ and everything He has for us.
   • Describe your version of a prosperous and successful life.
   • How can we do all the right things for all the wrong reasons when we pursue a prosperous life?
   • Read aloud Philippians 3:4b-9a and discuss the ways that Paul encourages us to forget about standing on our pedigrees or accomplishments and begin to stand in Christ as we pursue the life to which God has called us.

9. My mother said that when people tell us to "hang in there," we shouldn't listen to them. When we're hanging in there, we are vulnerable, exposed, and susceptible to our weaknesses. That's not where we want to be! She said believers are called to bravely stand in there with our full armor of God and stand firm no matter what comes our way.

# Notes

- How do these words from my mother encourage you to boldly face the work to which God has called you?
- What do you think the difference is between hanging in there and standing in there?
- How can you stand firm in the call upon your life no matter what comes your way?

10. You can't be who you want to be without being who God made you to be. Remember whose you are. You can do great things in Christ's name. Don't settle. Don't compromise. Let God nudge you into the place where you were meant to fit best, and then make your Father's name famous in the earth.
    - When have you tried to be something you are not?
    - How hard is it to let go of what we thought we were supposed to be in order to embrace who God made us to be?
    - Describe a time when you had a clear revelation about a unique gift, ability, or desire God has placed in you.
    - How can you use your gifts and abilities to make God famous in the earth?

## Be About His Love (5 minutes; Extended Option 10 minutes)

Ask everyone to turn to a neighbor to talk about a particular challenge from the Be About His Love section of the weekly readings. Say something like this: *On Day 5 you wrote I Know statements as you read more promises God has made to His beloved children. Share with your neighbor the I Know statements you discovered as you let God's promises wash over you during the week.*

### Extended Option

Have a discussion about the ways in which gifts, dreams, and visions have been stirred up in the lives of each participant. Tell a story about when you boldly stepped into your lane of purpose. Invite the ladies to identify what it means for them to step into the spotlight and shine for Jesus in their own unique way.

## Embrace His Love (5 minutes; Extended Option 10-15 minutes)

Conclude the session with the music video "I Know." Introduce the video by inviting the women to surrender all of their gifts, talents, and dreams to the Lord as they listen to this song, singing along during the chorus.

Play the music video (5:00 minutes). Then pray this prayer or one of your own:

*Sweet heavenly Father,*
*We thank You for embracing us in Your love today and for moving in our hearts. Lord we pray that our lives would bring You glory, that our work would be excellent as if every task was just for You. Call us, Lord. Equip us. Give us courage to accomplish Your purpose for our lives. Give us a vision of who we were meant to be. And God, we will give You all the praise for any good thing that comes our way. In fact, we will praise You no matter what, because even when we can't see we know You are*

# Notes

*always working all things together for our good. We love You, Lord. We thank You in advance for what You're going to do in and through each of us. Fill us up and send us out. We pray in Jesus' name. Amen.*

### Extended Option

After showing the closing music video, invite the women to divide into small groups of three to four and complete this sentence, "I will live like I know I'm God's favorite by . . ." When each one has shared, invite them to share joys and concerns as well as highlights from their discoveries during the week and this session; then close in prayer together.

# Week 8

# YOU CAN LIVE *LOVED*

*Note: Time suggestions are modified for this session to allow sufficient time for the closing Embrace His Love activity.*

## Leader Preparation (Before the Session)

### Scripture Focus
*"Embrace this God-life. Really embrace it, and nothing will be too much for you."*
Mark 11:22 *THE MESSAGE*

### Key Bible Story
When we fully accept and return God's embrace, we find that we are filled with promise, blessing, and purpose. We are able to conquer our fears, gain victory in our battles, and see prosperity. The Gospel of Mark reminds us that when we live in the kingdom of God, we can be sure that He will supply our needs and give us strength to face anything that comes our way.

He is Abba, a daddy to those who need a Father. He is the gentle Shepherd to those who long for tender care. If your life needs resolution, He is the God who can do exceedingly abundantly above all that we can even ask or think. If you have a problem, He is the problem solver. If you are facing a mountain that seems too high or a valley that seems too low, He is the Conqueror, and through Him nothing is impossible. He is Strength to the weak. He is Power to the powerless. He is Hope to the hopeless. He is Peace in the midst of the storm. He is Assurance in the midnight hour. And He is Joy in the morning. Truly, when we fall into God's embrace, He is everything, everything we need, and nothing will be too much for us!

### Objective
Today you'll help your group learn that Jesus gives them everything they need to live *loved*.

### What You Will Need
- *Embraced by God* DVD and DVD player
- Cardstock and markers for each participant, a large sheet of paper or bulletin board and pins (Embrace His Love)

# Notes

## Warm Up to His Love (5 minutes; Extended Option 10 minutes)

### Welcome Activity

Welcome participants and go around the room and have each participant share something that she discovered about God or her relationship with God during this study.

### Extended Option

Ask the women to revisit the idea of being God's favorite. Have them turn to their neighbor and talk about how this awesome truth has deepened their relationship with God.

### Recite the Memory Verse

By now your group has probably committed to memory John 17:23 and hidden this beautiful truth deep in your hearts. Write the verse on a board or flip chart. Read aloud the entire passage and emphasize the words *"you loved them just as much as you loved me,"* speaking that phrase a little louder than the rest of the passage. Then erase the board or flip the chart and recite the verse together from memory, again emphasizing the same phrase.

*"I will be in them and you will be in me so that they will be completely one. Then the world will know that you sent me and that **you loved them just as much as you loved me.**"*
John 17:23 NCV

### Opening Prayer

Pray this prayer or one of your own to begin your study today:

*Dear heavenly Father,*

*Wow! What a journey of discovery this has been. We thank You, Lord, that You have been with us every step of the way. We thank You that You open wide Your arms and enfold us in Your warm embrace. John 3:16 says You so love us! And we desire to so love You in return. What a joy to live our lives as an expression of Your love, knowing that You love us just as much as Your Son, Jesus. Now, Lord, we pray that You would ignite in us a passion. And every day we will practice living* loved *so that everything we do is an outpouring of who You are in us. We want our lives to be a love song to You. In Your name we pray. Amen.*

### Weekly Reading Recap

- To live *loved*, we desire to sow love everywhere we go. The more we give, the more love we sow.
- To live *loved*, we desire to stay connected to the Vine.
- On hard days, we can live *loved* by remaining constantly and consciously aware of God's loving presence.
- We live *loved* by surrounding ourselves with sisters who will build us up, encourage us, and cheer us on in our love walk with God.
- We live *loved* by continually giving more and more of ourselves to Jesus.

## Bask in His Love (15-20 minutes)

Play the Week 8 video segment on the DVD. Invite participants to complete the Video Viewer Guide for Week 8 in the participant book as they watch.

# Notes

## Talk About His Love (15 minutes; Extended Option 25 minutes)

**Discussion Points**

1. You can live *loved* by being fully confident that God's love for you will never fail. You can live *loved* by standing firmly on what you know, not on what you feel. You can live *loved* by being a blessing and shining a light everywhere you go. You can live *loved* by confidently living out God's wonderful plan and purpose for you. You can live *loved* when you give God all the praise and glory for the wonderful life He has set before you.
   - What does it look like to be fully confident that God's love will never fail?
   - Describe what it means to stand firmly on what you know, not on what you feel.
   - Name some ways that you can be a blessing and shine a light wherever you go.
   - In what ways have you begun to live out God's wonderful plan and purpose for you?
   - What is happening now in your life for which you give God all the praise and glory?

2. You're either a missionary or a mission project. The difference is that missionaries know what it means to develop a lifestyle of giving. Just like a body of water grows stagnant if it has no outlet, the same is true of our lives. Even if your efforts are small, little things will make a big difference. Missionaries understand this well.
   - When have you felt like a missionary?
   - When have you felt like someone's mission project?
   - How can you make small and large efforts to give what you can?

3. Ask a volunteer to read aloud Mark 11:22-24. Then read it from *THE MESSAGE:*

   *Embrace this God-life. Really embrace it, and nothing will be too much for you. This mountain, for instance: Just say, "Go jump in the lake"—no shuffling or shilly-shallying—and it's as good as done. That's why I urge you to pray for absolutely everything, ranging from small to large. Include everything as you embrace this God-life, and you'll get God's everything.*

   - What does it mean to get God's everything?
   - What does it mean to embrace this God-life?
   - Can you imagine embracing God so much that you can move mountains? What would it take to have that kind of faith?

4. Ask participants to form small groups of 3-4. Refer them to Day 1 and the study of 1 Peter 3:8-11. Have them discuss the prayers that they wrote based on the

# Notes

passage and the areas they need to keep praying about. Then bring the groups back together for more discussion.

- How hard was it to turn 1 Peter 3:8-11 into prayers?
- What common themes came up in your prayers?
- What do you think you most need to work on and pray about?
- How would living this way be an expression of living the God life?

5. When we are connected to the life source, we thrive and flourish with the fruit of our growth. If we become separated from the Vine, then our spiritual lives bear no fruit and wither up.
    - What fruit comes from someone who is connected to the Vine (Jesus)? (Direct them to their vine drawings in Day 2.)
    - How do we stay connected to the Vine?
    - When have you felt like you were withering up?
    - When have you felt like you were growing and thriving?

6. In a world where far too many people have forgotten about God, and even more have forgotten that He loves them, determine to be one of those who will rise high above the crowd and shout from the mountaintop: There is a great big God, and His love is available for the whole wide world!
    - Who in your life is far from God?
    - How does your life demonstrate to them that God is good and He loves them?
    - How does your life shout from the mountaintop that God's love is available for the whole wide world?

7. Don't let anything come between you and God's love for you. Don't let guilt separate you. Don't let shame separate you. Don't let your past mistakes separate you. Don't let anything separate you from God's love.
    - How do guilt and past mistakes make us feel like we are separated from God?
    - Read Romans 8:35, 37-39 aloud. What does Paul say about what separates us from God? Share your versions of these verses you wrote on Day 3.
    - When you get down and discouraged, how does this passage encourage you to fall into God's embrace?

8. When we return God's embrace we find that He is everything we need.
    - When you think about what you need, what is on that list?
    - How does God meet those needs?
    - How is it that nothing will ever be too much for us when we fully embrace the God-life?
    - What excites you about fully embracing the God-life?

## Be About His Love (5 minutes; Extended Option 10 minutes)

Ask everyone to turn to a neighbor to talk about a particular challenge from the Be About His Love section of the weekly readings. Say something like this: *On Day 1 you were challenged to perform a random act of kindness. Talk with your neighbor about that experience and how easy or difficult it would be to practice random acts of kindness more frequently.*

## Embrace His Love (20 minutes; Extended Option 25 minutes)

Today's closing will be a little different because you will have a special time of worship together as you end this study. Show the music video "The Love of God" one time as the group watches (6:01 minutes). Then, hand out sheets of cardstock or poster boards and markers to each participant and invite the women to write cardboard testimonies. Ask them to consider all that they have discovered about who they are and who God is over the course of these last eight weeks. Encourage them to look deep into their hearts to see what God has done in them and how God has called them to respond. On one side of the cardstock or poster board they are to write a sentence or two about their faith, life, or personal experience before they experienced God's embrace, and on the other side they are to write a sentence or two about their faith, life, or personal experience after accepting God's embrace. (Tell them not to write their names on them.) While the women are working, play "The Love of God" music video one or more times.

When participants have completed their testimonies, explain that you are going to play some music and as they feel led, they may stand up one at a time to show their cardboard testimonies. Depending on the configuration of the room, each woman may want to stand by her chair or come before the group at the front of the room. She is to hold up the "before" side of her testimony and then flip it to the "after" side. After each woman holds up her testimony, encourage the group to clap in praise for what God has done. Play the music video "The Love of God" or the *Embrace* CD as background music for this time of testimony. (Consider displaying the "after" sides of the testimonies in the room or another space for a designated time period after the study.)

### *The Declaration*

Invite the women to open their participant books to The Declaration (page 207) and stand as you lead them in a special declaration of who they are in Christ. Say something like this: *As we close our time together, let's declare that we belong to God and long to live fully for Him with confidence and courage, fulfilling the purpose God prepared in advance for us. Now we will recite together The Declaration as a public profession of our ongoing commitment to continually give our lives to Jesus.*

# Notes

# Notes

## The Declaration

### I Am a Daughter of the Most High King

I am a daughter of the Most High King. I am deeply loved, highly favored, and greatly blessed. My identity is in Christ alone. I know who I am and Whose I am. I am the righteousness of God in Christ. I am accepted in the Beloved and a joint heir together with Him. I am a part of the Family of God and the Holy Spirit dwells in me.

I will follow Jesus with all my heart. There will be no turning around, no slacking up, no backing down, no striking out, and no giving in. I will not compromise my faith, lower my standards, or cower in the face of adversity. My past is forgiven. My present has purpose, and my best and brightest days are still ahead of me. I walk by faith and not by sight. My gaze is fixed and my mind is made up. I am determined not to think like the world, walk like the world, talk like the world, or act like the world. I shall not be moved. I cannot be shaken. And I will not be swayed. I belong to Jesus and I set my sights on things above. Earth is my mission and Heaven is my destiny.

I confess that I can do all things through Christ Who strengthens me. All things are possible. So if God is for me, who can be against me? My faith is rooted and established in love, and nothing I have done or ever will do can ever diminish the height, the depth, the length, and the breadth of God's love for me. I am convinced that neither death, nor life, angels or demons, the present, the future, or any powers will be able to separate me from the love of God, which is in Christ Jesus our Lord.

I eagerly await Christ's return. And on that great day He will know me and call me by name. His banner over me is love, and I will lift my voice in loudest hallelujahs to sing His praises forevermore. For I am a daughter of the Most High King!

Close by saying this prayer or one of your own:

*Sweet heavenly Father,*

*We thank You for embracing us in Your love each time we have gathered in Your name and for the way that You have moved in our hearts. God, as we go from this place and live out all that we have learned about Your embrace on our lives, we pray that you would embolden us, strengthen us, and equip us to do all that You have made us to do.*

*Lord, we give You praise for all You've done and all You're going to do. We want to make Your name famous in all the earth. Let our lives point to You and shine Your bright light of love to anyone who looks our way. We love You, Lord, and we thank You for who You are. You are so very good to us. In Jesus' name, we pray. Amen.*

### *Extended Option*

Invite the group to share joys and concerns as they lift up prayers for one another.

Notes

# Leader Helps

## Preparing for the sessions . . .

- Decide whether you will use the 60-minute or 90-minute format option. Be sure to communicate dates and times to participants in advance.
- Distribute participant books to all members at least one week before your first session and instruct them to complete the first week's readings. If you have the phone numbers or e-mail addresses of your group members, send out a reminder and a welcome.
- Check out your meeting space before each group session. Make sure the room is ready. Do you have enough chairs? Do you have the equipment and supplies you need? (See the list of materials needed in each session outline.)
- Pray for your group and each group member by name. Ask God to work in the life of every woman in your group.
- Read and complete the week's readings in the participant book and review the session outline in the leader guide. Select the discussion points and questions you want to cover and make some notes in the margins to share in your discussion time.

## Leading the sessions . . .

- Personally welcome and greet each woman as she arrives. Have everyone sign the group roster (see page 61).
- At the start of each session, ask the women to turn off or silence their cell phones.
- Always start on time. Honor the time of those who are on time.
- Encourage everyone to participate fully, but don't put anyone on the spot. Invite the women to share as they are comfortable. Be prepared to offer a personal example or answer if no one else responds at first.
- Communicate the importance of completing the weekly readings and participating in group discussion.
- Facilitate but don't dominate. Remember that if you talk most of the time, group members may tend to listen rather than to engage. Your task is to encourage conversation and keep the discussion moving.
- If someone monopolizes the conversation, kindly thank her for sharing and ask if anyone else has any insights.

# Notes

- Try not to interrupt, judge, or minimize anyone's comments or input.
- Remember that you are not expected to be the expert or have all the answers. Acknowledge that all of you are on this journey together, with the Holy Spirit as your leader and guide. If issues or questions arise that you don't feel equipped to handle or answer, talk with the pastor or a staff member at your church.
- Don't rush to fill the silence. If no one speaks right away, it's okay to wait for someone to answer. After a moment, ask, "Would anyone be willing to share?" If no one responds, try asking the question again a different way—or offer a brief response and ask if anyone has anything to add.
- Encourage good discussion, but don't be timid about calling time on a particular question and moving ahead. Part of your responsibility is to keep the group on track. If you decide to spend extra time on a given question or activity, consider skipping or spending less time on another question or activity in order to stay on schedule.
- Try to end on time. If you are running over, give members the opportunity to leave if they need to. Then wrap up as quickly as you can.
- Thank the women for coming and let them know you're looking forward to seeing them next time.
- Be prepared for some women to want to hang out and talk at the end. If you need everyone to leave by a certain time, communicate this at the beginning of the group session. If you are meeting in a church during regularly scheduled activities, be aware of nursery closing times.

# Group Roster

Notes

| Name | Phone Number | E-mail |
|------|--------------|--------|
| 1. | | |
| 2. | | |
| 3. | | |
| 4. | | |
| 5. | | |
| 6. | | |
| 7. | | |
| 8. | | |
| 9. | | |
| 10. | | |
| 11. | | |
| 12. | | |
| 13. | | |
| 14. | | |
| 15. | | |

For Babbie's latest concert and event information
and for ordering *Embrace* and other CDs,
visit www.babbie.com.

*You also can follow Babbie on Facebook and Twitter.*

# Combining Christian Fiction and Bible Study

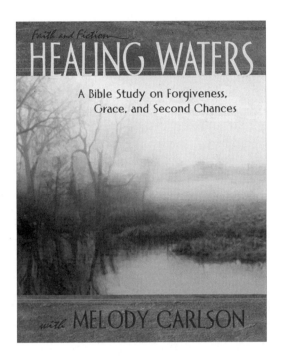

Popular Christian fiction author Melody Carlson draws upon her novels in the Inn at Shining Waters Series to invite women on an exciting journey toward healing. Using the stories, themes, and characters of the novels as a backdrop, this eight-week study explores the need for forgiveness and mercy in our lives and the role that second chances and new beginnings play in healing our spirits and relationships.

Abingdon Press / August 2012

For more information
visit AbingdonPress.com
or your favorite Christian retailer.